AF242095

Absolutely
Always

Published by Friendly Monster Press - Portland, Oregon, USA
friendlymonsterpress.com
ISBN: 978-1-967814-01-5

Absolutely Always

POEMS ABOUT LOVE

ERIN CLARKE

For Taylor and the boys

Table of Contents

Absolutely Always

I can't be sure because I am sure
Of almost nothing,
But perhaps a way to save the world
Is to love it,
Truly love it:

Love the world so much you cannot stand by and watch it hurting,
but instead
Hold it closer,
Hold it dearly, draw it in like it's your best friend
Freshly dumped on New Year's,
Hold it all like your baby, like a puppy, like your childhood self alone and in
dire need of hugs.

I will never say I'm sorry for loving marshmallows in hot chocolate,
Or the moss under the bus bench,
Or the feel of sassy boots,
Because this practice of loving
Is, indeed, my power—it is all I have against the wounds
Bleeding so far out of reach,
It is what keeps me breathing in this smog of endless unprecendentations,
Snarled among the tenacious long-fingered roots of cruelty.

So yes, I will love books I will love bubbles I will love brownies I will love
you,
I will love and
I will fight because I love,

Keep loving no matter what, absolutely always,

It's what makes humans worth being.

Him

Married, 10 years in

The deepest love I ever felt
was a warmth, a
melting in my core—not like butter on a skillet, mind,
more like cast iron buckling into relieved molten freedom,
relaxing into softness,
a swell welling up as you
sat—entirely engaged
in something on a screen,
oblivious that I was noticing
your place in the universe
(and radiating gratitude that it is so near mine).

There were no flowers,
sonnets, harps, or fanfare.
No background music, no grand gestures of planned devotion.

There was worn carpet,
an easy chair,
the rhythmic clank of a
zipper in the dryer.

The sweep of the feeling
lasted only a few breaths, then
faded into story,
yet the overwhelming approval
of everything
about you
lingered like fragrance, coloring the room.

Love Story Origins

Some people still ask
how our love came to be,
and why the
certainty in choosing you
rivaled the unbreakable self-assurance
of a rock's own timelessness.
It's a tricky thing to answer

For to describe
what you are to me,
first I must remember
the feeling of being
split
into pieces
for everyone's convenience—
less a woman
than a drugstore snack pack.

They'd peel open my wrapper
and my wax-lined mouth would flap
as a hijacked puppet,
filling in the blanks
of the story written for me
by unsolicited ghosts,
feeding me my lines.
With revulsion I would hear
my own precious words
warped by prisms of perception,
edited into narratives not of my writing,
and I could never scoop them back
out of those strangers' minds.

These were my connections
with humankind

until I met you.

You had no plans,
made up no stories,
held no assumptions, shaded me through no filters.
You had no containers to fill,
no roles for me to play.

You listened.
You loved.

For so long I was
a series
of one-dimensional characters.

With you
I am myself;
the full gnarled junkheap of messes stacked on messes,
every angle of me beloved,
every note of me savored
like an infinitely complex wine.

So really,
dear reader,
tell me something true.
If you had one like him,
wouldn't you marry him too?

11 Things I Can't Get Enough of With This Guy

1.) When he falls asleep he looks like a Vermeer painting, all gentle slopes and luminous skin.

2.) His Scooby-Doo laugh; it's not a bit, that's really how it sounds, how it tumbles out all chortles and breathy cartoon guffaws.

3.) How he looks in a baseball tee. (I dunno why, but it works for me.)

4.) The fact that he's 6ft, broad-built, and bearded, yet sneezes like a teeny kitten. (It's been 14 years, and it's still funny every time.)

5.) His warm and bright singing voice—like mahogany-polished sunshine expanding throughout the house in resonant floating tones.

6.) Cliché, but have you seen his eyes? And seen his eyes seeing your eyes with their velvet brown intrepid, holding you sweetly in his gaze?

7.) That he says yes to any and all pastry quests.

8.) How the depth of his patience makes the Pacific look like a baby pool.

9.) The photos he texts me from the road: dogs he meets, funny signs, excitement over snails—pure enthusiasm in every pixel lighting up my dreary phone.

10.) The way he gets worked up at any given selfishness—when systems are unkind and the hurt are left still hurting—because he honestly believes that we are better than this. And while he vents his ire, airing righteous indignation, it kind of makes me believe it too.

11.) The feel of his hand
      in my hand
            on the couch
while we sit doing blissful, endless, nothing.

Tied Down

Lock me in your bedframe arms
Bind me with a heavy ring
Wrap me in tasks
With firm due dates
And baby let's share paperwork together,
You and me
And exhaustion
And trauma
And newsreels
And little feet that keep getting bigger,
Rubbing rubber right off the
Soles dragged as brakes
On the concrete all summer,
So that's another new pair of shoes then already, huh?
We pay for it in daily devoted
Breakfast dances passing
Endless orange juice
And texted conversations
So the children can't hear
Our worry, can't hear the weight
In our voices as we bear it all
Between us,
Baring bodies on occasion,
Slipping sideways into sleep,
Hold me tighter
Like a bandage
So I know I'm held at all.

Monday, Dinner

Once there was a day
you caught me scratching my boob by
reaching underneath my dress
for better access,
skirt hiked to the ribs
and elbow jutting out
in what must have been an utterly ridiculous angle
as I absently skimmed a recipe for Pineapple Curry,
and you
laughed 'til you cried,
and later told me I was your
dream girl
all over again,
and I only wish I knew how to make a billion of you
so everyone alive
can be this loved.

Strings

I see you, marionette man,
Elevated suspended and tethered,
These cords that yank at uncomfortable angles
Anchored to agendas,
Or withering like cobwebs drifting
Unmoored from
Whatever long-left purpose.

As I watch you
With one shoulder askew,
Knees lifting on your way to the next task on the list,
I long to give you a large pair of scissors
And permission to let it all drop

He Tries

I really couldn't love you more
But somehow I did
That day you came home, shaken
Heavy-gray like all the sorrows
Of the earth were borne upon your lonely back.

I asked you what was wrong,
And you told me the story.
You saw a woman walk straight into a busy road
And sit down in the traffic,
Waiting to die.

So many drove right past
And so you did a u-turn,
Parked crossways in front of her
To keep her safe, for now;
The cops came shortly after,
You were told that you could go.

You dragged yourself home, devastated,
And all you asked was why—
Why did no one else help her?
You didn't know what to do,
You did only what you could think of
Knowing it wouldn't be enough.

I loved you so much more that day,
My heart breaking bigger to hold
The wounded shards of yours,
Because you didn't see:
Those who kept driving didn't know what to do either.
They couldn't face the unknown and risk to be found wanting.
But you, my dearest,
Even clueless and half-doomed, your darling soul made you try.
So help me, I love a man who tries.

Waking, Sunday Morning

Reaching across the unfurled cozy sea,
finding an island of shoulders,
and chest, nestling nose into quiet—
the glen between chin and neck
edged with jaw—
currents beating softly under the surface of warmth,
my homestay afloat on memory foam.
Breathe and be,
it's enough for me.

Ours

You'll notice I don't have any poems about sex,
Because some things are only ours—
Like the poem I wrote for you no one else will ever see,
And the road trip hums you sing no else will ever hear,
And that thing you said that made laugh so hard I fell off the couch—
I can't recall the joke,
But I recall the falling
And the hot streaks of mirth-tears glistening on my cheeks while I shook
with soundless laughter on the floor.
Some things are only ours to keep
Away from all others—
Like mumbled nonsense in your sleep
And the way I look at breakfast—
We secret our best moments
Cloaked in private
Drenched in code,
Being ours,
Only ours,
Only ours.

Them

How are you even here

There was nothing and then there were
Shoulder blades,
Tiny ones that spanned my thumb's length
Jutting beneath your silky surface
And I obsessed over your angles hidden in the curves.
There's a blur of socks and wailing
And sticky fruit on shoes, walls,
Sleep during the movie,
And precious snores through tiny slack-jawed mouths—
Only a handful of moments make it out of the murk
To survive in memory, not photo,
The real full remembering
Of rocking you in my arms,
Bouncing with you on our secondary blue planet made of rubber,
Soaking in each inch of your ever-changing face.
Let me drink your breath
Just a little longer,
I'll give it back, I know it's yours,
But please, stay wrapped in my elbow crook
Just a little longer,
I have to know this thing I made
That contentedly hums to itself in rooms alone
Is unapologetically, actually, real.

Honey Bunny

He was my first eternal love,
That darling dreamy boy
With alien eyes and rabbit feet
Bundled in apple-printed velcro sacs,
He outgrew them instantly
To be a soft-sided Lego boy—
All chunky squares and gleeful grins
Hoarding balloons and books in bed
Like a builder hoards good lumber;
The books were roads, ladders,
Towers, hats, blankets,
Even stories sometimes—
In between readings the legs tripled
The neck stretched, the arms lanked:
A butterbean to a string bean,
"Don't call me that," he said, eyes red,
So Butterbean he stayed, from the first day to forever, now
A full-grown full-speed hare,
Fast as lightning, brows deep
In the books again–only for reading, these days–
Curled up with his tender heart fluttering under
Spindly basket ribs,
Our short-tempered philosopher
Whose comforts are equations in which
Everything makes sense and all
Variables are controlled,
Plus his chaos-muppet mother
Nuzzling his cheek
'Til he blushes, but he loves it—he loves me,
With absolutely no idea how much I love him more.

Soundscape: Contentment

The oscillating whoosh of the dishwasher's
jets of water swirling in repetitive orbits,

The syncopated rhythm of
lift,
sip,
replace
the mug on the side table,
breathe, pause,
repeat,

The sporadic thumps of leaps,
bounds, and collisions
of preschool limbs on every surface,

"Can you hear this?"
In wonderment he spins a craft-abandoned glitter-elastic
so fast it makes a vhoo vhoo vhoo
with each circumlocution too fast to see,

lift,
sip,
replace,
watch the spritzing freezing rain
needling the shingles outside,

The whisper, "Mommy? I want to snuggle with you,"
and the ensuing rustle of t-shirt on sweatshirt,
leggings on jeans as he climbs up,
folding his too-long limbs into my
same-sized lap, curling up with me
under a quiet blanket
we watch the sky outside,
and the dishwasher continues
keeping whooshing time.

These are the sounds of my deepest happiness.

Aggrieved

Grief sits heavy on the chest
Creeping into quieted throat,
Tightening its reins,
Swallowing my true sounds.
The dead weight on ribs
Compacting inner bits
Into harder, denser tissue,

This labor one's penance
For the risk of loving.

It will sit forever if I let it—
Grief has no manners of its own,
And we don't like to look at
Such a hideous thing;
The creature wrought
From empty spaces
Of hope lost,
The thing that cries
"It hurts"
In muffled croaking stabs,
It hurts it hurts it hurts to be alive
And care.

My caring kicks me in the teeth,
Like my toddler slapping my face,
Clawing my arm, lashing out with his tiny body,
So explosive is his rage and hate,

But I keep caring under the weight
And sting, drawing shaky breaths while staring deep
In the reddened eyes
Of Grief, still loving
Absolutely always,

This is the work, my guardian spell so
I do not become
The hollowed choking monster
Myself.

The Good Shit

I dream of bottling your laughter, in all its varieties and vintages.
The light bubbling giggles.
The high, swooping whoops of surprise, like a gull
thrilled to have discovered
an unexpected snack.
The drawn-out gliding chorus of a single vowel as you two stare
at each other,
bonding over something we've completely missed.
The squeaky chortles.
The bold punch HA!s
But my favorite,
the ones I'll savor 'til my dying day,
are the rumblings that emanate from your center,
a seismic joy,
so strong it vibrates chuckles through your whole shaking body
and you couldn't stop them if you tried.

Those I would capture and seal to hoard in bunkers
like bags of grain for the end of days,
knowing that your uncontrollable laughter
makes everything since my first breath
worth it.

Motherwork

Prove you love me again.
The 72nd time today. This morning. This hour.
Help me with the faucet I can already reach.
Be on my side.
Bring me some juice.
Respond immediately to my thoughts.
Pull up my pants.
Not him, you.
Prove you love me.
(Remind me I am loved.)
Tell me you'll do anything,
any hour,
again and again
and again and again until I decide
I hate you.
In return you may have my laughter,
and my wit,
and my hugs,
and the honor of cleaning up my vast puddles of urine.
(You're welcome.)
Thank you for your service.
Now prove you love me again.

Starboy

The absolute jazz of it

I cannot begin to tell it all on high:

How you gently hold a gifted rose by the thorns,

How you belt names of states with the tenacious lungs of a Broadway
brat,

How your cape leaves sparkles on the carpet, twinkle tracks tracing your
paths,

How to you I am the best in the world,

And to me you are the best in the world

And together we cannot grasp the gushing rainbow glow like lava

But I can touch your face and melt in it

My spectacular child,

The atoms that gathered to be your beating heart

Were waiting for this, I can tell,

The stars are proud to have become you

And my god I get to watch it all, the absolute jazz of it,

While all I can say is "I love you" every day,

Never enough.

Jigsaw Puzzle

Knees curled on top
of curled knees
nestling in my
belly, inverse stairs
that fit in our Tetris love,
elbow rests on
lip and I feel
your bones waiting
under skin, the
pits and grooves of
joints in this atypical
prolonged dry kiss.
Heart and heart,
a life from a life,
you climb on my side,
draped over my
mountain range of
shoulder and hip
with your angles
everywhere,
your impossibly soft
cheek on my eye,
breath warming my nose
in locomotor puffs,
the giggles of morning
and creaking of my
articulations
the only offering
available to honor
this fleeting moment
your body matches mine
in a love so perfect
it kindles a long-dark
cold-bricked fireplace of
happiness long forgotten.

Nightmares in the racecar bed

You call me, hunted by self-made demons,
My fibers are taut with agony as I hear you

Screaming for mercy,
Begging for comfort from your

Haunted room.
How can I reach you,

Your mind the oubliette, my dearest darling's
Genius hijacked by horror—

I would scale rocky cliffs
With bloodied nails to keep

You safe—with no such tangible challenge my
Furor and panic snort and foam, white-eyed.

Climb down and be with me,
Safe, and feather-light,

Where I can fold my arms around your form and
Soften your quaking.

Come home to me,
Come home to me please,

I cannot don invisible armor
And gut those conjured monsters

With any steel known
So please baby, please come home.

Slow Mo

Every season you grow
more angled,
corners rising
from the round soft deep.
The sweet collection of ovals
that used to be you
turning into a detailed
geometric sculpture,
a man in miniature.

As sharp elbows unfurl,
your speckled bruised shins narrow
and lengthen,
I beg my faithless brain
Remember this, remember this.
The yawn, the kiss, the last whisper of belly,
the wobbling "r"s and stubby fingers
around my grateful hand.
Please, let me store this sensation
in the high-security vault
forever.

But alas, you always just look like you,
and any notion you were ever different
melts away like the rolls that used to
hug your knees and the contentment
you once had being strapped to my back—
an extension of my body that
happened to smile
at bouncing balls.

Ugh, fine, me I guess

Seasonally Affected

Once October falls
The good things aren't a given;
They are sought, courted, stalked
As a predator hunting lifeblood
Survives a starving wild.
I hoard hard-won treasures—fragments of fun—and build myself
A whimsy fortress under a drip-cloak of despair.
I tend my Hello Kitty bulwark
Against the pinching, slinking cold
As the slog bogs along
Night nipping at my edges.
The point being sometimes love looks like a dozen roses,
And other times it looks like a shit-ton of lamps
I bought at Goodwill back in August
Knowing soon
I will be desperate for the light.

A Love Poem About Standing

It took years of work
to find my feet.
To feel them comfortably
beneath my wayward body
and its perpetually teenaged face,
mismatching the exhausted dread
and the decades of hardened grief
that carved such deep channels
in my neural pathways.

Generations of glacial striae
stripped my mind, prepping
the area for survival battles
on the daily, weekly, yearly, hourly.

Depression:
The sensation of every emotion
shoved down with such force
the body becomes dense,
like a kettlebell, and
opening the eyes
becomes a daily weight-lifting regimen.

Anxiety:
A swirling bubblewind in which
nothing is safe, stationary,
or even existing longer
than it takes to gasp a shallow
breath before the next tries
to skitter away from grasping lungs.

Financial Insecurity:
Eight syllables to convey
a rug being pulled out beneath you
every day, always, and
on the way down
filling out forms read by
overworked skeptics

who judge whether or not
you're really trying not to fall.

And here I am.
My third decade.
All toes wiggling, soaking up
the weight of me.
My face indefinably
rougher, middle jigglier,
arms weaker, hips wider,
movements slower.

But in the full-length mirror,
There she is.
A grown-ass woman,
Still standing.

Summer 1997

As a habitual small blonde thing I scaled
The tree in the backyard to sing,

Like somehow the height afforded privacy,
The distance my permission slip,

Those vast swaths of thin air between me
And the ground a buffer zone catching and turning back

Judgment or annoyed ears,
Once I was perched it was my world, only mine,

A place of pure pleasure,
And what pleased me most was singing

Whatever songs I knew
Out to the clouds

For the sheer sound of sound joining the chorus of
Thrumming cicadas and creaking wood

In the summer breezes,
Dirt speckling the hollows of my knees

As they were slung over branches,
At least one fresh pink-striped scrape

On some part of my freckled limbs,
At least one ant tickling my ankle as it mistook me for bark,

The dancing millions of
Oval-shaped leaves

On thousand fingered twigs
Catching sun rays and shining electric green,

Salt sweat on my lip
And streaks in my hair where UVs bleached me golden white,

I sang for the vibrations in my chest
And the sweet quiet after,

The space welling in my absence a fascination
While the tree waved tipsy

And my mother tried not to look—
She was afraid of heights

And afraid of me not being afraid of heights—
I never considered I would fall,

It crossed my mind
As often as fear of falling from a rug to the floor,

Which is to say never,
I knew the tree would hold me

For I was dear
To the world
When I sang in the tree.

Or hardly working

It might be called masochism
But I take pride in blisters,
They comfort me like a pat on the back
By a large dry hand
Because blisters
Are participation awards
Garnered by attempting the new—
Or old with new vigor,
Their vinegar bite heralding a bold change,
Movement, progress,
A labor wrought with muscle and skin
With strength enough to burst an upper layer of self
In a sigh of tender fluid,
Blisters are for the brave
Wearers of inappropriate shoes
And forgetters of work gloves
And others who let their soft surface
Rip away in tiny bits
To become something challenged,
Callused and wisened,
Amassing temporary tree bark to defend against
The chafing world.
It might be called masochism
But I love my blisters,
They remind me I'm still trying.

Crybaby

Almost anything turns on the faucet
But it's usually exhaustion
That wends its way through lacrimal portals
Easing rancor from my ragged brain—
Drips unwinding wire shoulders,
Pit-pat droplets of mimicked rain
Wash free the detritus of grit and grief
So my heart can cavort again,
Serenity swimming up to fill the space
Loosened of barbed memory and stale self-abuse.
It's worth the splotchy face
And anxious glances—
Sometimes, baby, you've just gotta wail
To make room for all the rest.

You

Life's Work

Let enthusiasm shake you
Sing at breakfast
Cackle loudly
Share the meme
Hug the pillow
Binge the read
Eat the donut
Coo with full-throated ardor over beautiful little things
Be contagiously courageous
You can do it and you should—
You're a walking squishy dreamthing
Sustained by your own believing—
Smooch the kitten
Love the sky
This is why
We're here.

Acknowledgements

The poem "Honey Bunny" was previously published in the collection, *Fortnight* (Picture Frame Press), thank you to all the collaborators on that project.
"Waking, Sunday Morning" was previously published in the e-zine, *Home Coming Queen*, by me, so we're not too worried about it.

The existence of this book is largely due to the support, enthusiasm, and expertise of Scott Cannon, without whom all of this would still be a jumble of old Google Docs. If you liked this book, please send him a psychic high-five.

Huge thanks to all the early readers who sent me words of encouragement; especially to those kind enough to write about this work in the form of promotional blurbs. "Blurb" is a very silly word, but the act of creating one is such an incredible gift from one writer to another, and I am deeply grateful. Also thanks to the on-time and later readers: your presence is a gift too.

I give endless thanks to my husband, Taylor, who graciously agreed to love me forever with no takebacksies. Thanks are also due to our amazing sons for allowing me to brag about them publicly in ways that will definitely be embarrassing later. (Sorry about the urine comment, btw.)

Lastly, a word of appreciation for my cat Mochi who kept my lap warm through every stage of the editing process. Maybe now that she is included in the book she will stop chewing on my pens.

About the Author

Erin Clarke is a poet, linguist, and massage therapist. Her first book, *(Im)perfect Blooms* was published in 2023, and her writing has been featured in *Wellspring Literary Magazine, The Pointed Circle, Bellwether Review,* and elsewhere. She resides in Portland, Oregon with her husband, their two children, and a very floofy cat. You can read more of her work at erinclarkewrites.com.